MASTERING THE FIVE MANAGERIAL SUPERPOWERS

By Jennifer Hancock

Published by Jennifer Hancock

Copyright 2024 by Jennifer Hancock

Published 2024

Edition: Paperback Edition

ISBN: 9798336252453

Imprint: Independently published

Title: Mastering the Five Managerial Superpowers

Author: Jennifer Hancock

Editor: Desiree Vogelpohl

Publisher: Humanist Learning Systems

Word Count: 11,116

This book is also available in digital format at most online retailers

All rights reserved. No part of this book may be used or reproduced in any manner whatsoever without written permission, except in the case of brief quotations embodied in critical articles or reviews.

CONTENTS

CHAPTER 1: THE 5 MANAGERIAL SUPERPOWERS   7

CHAPTER 2: SELF AWARENESS: THE FOUNDATION OF EFFECTIVE MANAGEMENT   13

CHAPTER 3: MANAGING CHANGE AND TRANSITIONS   25

CHAPTER 4: TAKING OWNERSHIP   33

CHAPTER 5: CONFLICT MANAGEMENT   41

CHAPTER 6: MANAGING PEOPLE   57

CHAPTER 7: LEADING BY EXAMPLE   63

CHAPTER 8: PRACTICAL APPLICATION AND IMPLEMENTATION   66

CHAPTER 9: CONCLUSION AND KEY TAKEAWAYS   69

CHAPTER 10: ABOUT THE AUTHOR   73

CHAPTER 1: THE 5 MANAGERIAL SUPERPOWERS

Mastering 5 managerial superpowers will help you learn how to navigate conflicts with grace, foster a positive work culture, and inspire your team to greatness. Gaining valuable soft skills in self-awareness, change management, conflict management, and effective communication will set you apart as a leader.

This book is designed to help you leverage the latest insights from behavioral science, and empower you to gain control over your responses, cultivate resilience, and become the influential leader you aspire to be. The key is to turn these skills into habits that drive success in your personal and professional life so you can unlock your full potential as a managerial superpower!

These 5 superpowers are the essential skills and strategies needed to excel in today's dynamic workplace.

What are the 5 Managerial Superpowers? What are the essential skills and strategies needed to excel in today's dynamic workplace?

1) The first superpower is self awareness. The only way to exercise control is to be in control of yourself. Self awareness is going to help you choose your actions strategically instead of just responding to the conditions you find yourself in. No other superpower is possible until or unless you have self control. You gain self control by becoming self aware.

2) The second superpower is the ability to manage change in yourself and others. No one likes change. The people who succeed are the ones who are able to control their response to change so that they can adapt more readily. The key to being able to do this is to understand why we all resist change and the behavioral science behind how change happens. This knowledge is going to help you manage change in yourself and others more effectively. Knowing this science and being

able to implement it is like having a superpower.

3) The third superpower is ownership and taking responsibility. Responsibility is the ability to choose your response. This is why self awareness is the first superpower. A leader is someone who has chosen to take responsibility to help their teams achieve more. Ownership in a humanistic management framework is a service oriented idea. We take responsibility or ownership to support others on our team. This is how we make sure the work gets done. It is not about doing it yourself. It is about taking ownership of your own choices and decisions and then doing the work needed to effectively support yourself and others.

4) The fourth superpower is conflict management. Managing people is difficult. Mostly because we, as humans, rarely agree. Understanding how to manage conflict and turn conflict into collaboration is a key skill. It

is at the heart of humanistic management. Just like change, there is science that can help you learn how to do this well, and once you know this, it is like having a superpower. This knowledge will change everything about how you approach people, disagreement, and deal with conflict among your team.

5) Finally, the fifth superpower is the ability to manage people and personalities. Humanistic management is about managing real live humans. It is no easy task. The previous superpowers were all leading up to this skill.

To manage people, you need to be self aware, you need to be able to choose your response, and adapt to change effectively and strategically. You need to take ownership of your actions and choose your actions wisely. So that you can manage conflict in a humanistic and scientific way so that your choices work.

All of that is going to help you manage people and whatever personalities you have to deal with –

with grace and dignity. Wouldn't it be nice to go through life with grace and your dignity intact? That is the superpower. You will not just be flopping around hoping for the best and failing. You will be a master of people management.

These skills build upon each other. For instance, you cannot manage change well without self awareness. You cannot manage conflict without the knowledge you need to manage change. And you cannot manage people until you know how to manage conflict. After you learn about the 5 superpowers and how they work and how to do them yourself, we are going to talk about how to practice these skills because they do require practice. And we are going to discuss how to apply them to your work and to your life.

CHAPTER 2: SELF AWARENESS: THE FOUNDATION OF EFFECTIVE MANAGEMENT

The first superpower is self awareness.

Self awareness is the foundation of effective management and it is the foundation of humanistic management. You cannot expect to be able to manage other humans if you cannot manage yourself. The only way to exercise control is to be in control of yourself so that you can choose your responses. Becoming self aware will help you not only understand yourself better, you will also understand your reactions and responses so that you can, hopefully, choose a response instead of just responding haphazardly and hoping for the best. As I said before, none of the other superpowers are possible until or unless you have self control. You gain self control by becoming self aware.

The Importance of Self Awareness in Management

If you have ever worked for a manager who was NOT in control of their responses, you understand how toxic those environments can be.

Managers who are not in control of how they respond force employees to manage the manager just so work can get done. It is an incredible drain on productivity. You end up spending half your time managing your manager instead of working. The manager is stealing productivity instead of increasing it. I personally never want to work for such a manager again, and I am sure you do not either.

Do not be that type of manager. Self awareness is the way to avoid being that type of manager. This is not just about emotional intelligence and communication. It is about self control. Self awareness is the first step to gaining self control.

You cannot control your response until you are aware of HOW you respond. This is not easy to do.

We all like to think we are in control of our thoughts and our actions, but we really are not. Our brains mostly run on autopilot. We become conscious of what is going on after the fact. Milliseconds, but still – after the fact.

Consciousness is a poorly understood thing. I recommend a book called: *The Thousand Brain Theory* by Jeff Hawkins (the guy who invented the Palm Pilot). His book explains what is happening in your brain to create consciousness really well. Basically, your neocortex is a pattern recognition device sitting atop a sensory input, primal drive, and emotional response brain. Your neocortex spends its time trying to make sense of all that. Consciousness, your awareness of what is happening, arises out of the neocortex trying to make sense of the inputs it is receiving. It does a pretty good job but it does get things wrong. It is important to know that your conscious brain can deceive you. What you think is happening may not actually be what is happening.

For instance, your brain can become absolutely convinced you are under a fatal attack when someone is just disagreeing with you. When this happens, your conscious brain goes – crap – I need to defend myself. When in reality, all you needed to do was listen and take in information that you needed to make a better decision. I know I have encountered people who respond like this. You probably have, too. I would be surprised if you have not also responded like this because I certainly have. Our emotions are great tools for helping us cope with the world, but they also can lead us astray. This is why self awareness is so important to being a super manager. It helps you respond rationally to stimulus instead of freaking out. It can also help you reset when your brain misleads you. But only if you are self aware.

Training Your Brain

How can you become emotionally intelligent if you are not already? Practice. Seriously, that is all that is required. The brain is super easy to hack.

The neocortex is a pattern recognition device. In order for it to learn a pattern, the pattern must be repeated. Daily, if possible, for just over a month.

Once the pattern is repeated enough, the brain starts lighting up and predicting the pattern and responding accordingly. That is the autopilot I was talking about. If you have ever been driving your car and you want to make a detour before going home, and you turn home instead of to the market, you have experienced this autopilot happening.

Your conscious decisions can override the autopilot, but it is pretty difficult to do. It takes time and repetition for the new pattern to get solidified in the structure of the brain. And, yes, it is a physical thing in the brain. It can be seen by scientists with the right equipment. Generally speaking, it takes about 30 days of steady practice for a new bit of learning to become solidified as a structure in the brain. Once it is, it will be easier to do whatever the skill is.

For example, my son's primitive reflexes did not integrate. The therapist had us do exercises with him twice a day every day for 30 days. Around day 28, suddenly the reflex integrated and he could do whatever the reflex was. It was almost like magic, except it was just basic brain science.

What Does This Mean for You – Who Want to Become More Self Aware

It means you need to practice it a lot, every day, for over a month. Here is what I want you to do. I want you to start noticing your emotions.

Check in with your emotions. When someone tells you to check your emotions, it may sound like an impossible task – like how am I NOT supposed to feel this strong emotion? It is the right emotion for what I am experiencing. That may be true. But that is not what checking your emotions is about. All it is, is the practice of becoming aware and conscious of what your emotions are. To do this, I want you to check in with your emotions a few times a day. Label them. Do not judge the emotions. Just label them. Hmmm – right now I am feeling a bit nervous and scared. Or – right now I am sad. Or - right now I am happy or tired or whatever. The more you do this when your emotions are minor, the easier it will be to do when your emotions are strong. The strong emotions are the sort of emotions that can get you out of control.

You do not need to think – why do I feel this? You are just labeling the emotion at this stage. The reason I do not want you to interrogate your emotions when you start is because it is not always possible to know why you feel a certain way. Sometimes, you just do. Our brains are sitting in a pool of chemicals and those chemicals – or lack of chemicals – impact our emotions. Sometimes the reason you are feeling anxious is because you are missing an important chemical. That is it.

Do not judge your emotions, do not try to not have the emotions. Just start labeling your emotions. Get in the practice of becoming aware of your emotions. What is happening in the brain when you do this is you are teaching your brain to think about emotions. After a bit, it will start doing this automatically and you will become more aware of what you are feeling.

Once you can do this reliably, the next step is to acknowledge the emotion – good or bad. Again, no judgment. Just acknowledge it. Once you can do that, then you can start training the brain to decide consciously what you want to do about whatever the emotion is. What action do you want to take based on your knowledge of your emotions? Sometimes doing nothing is the best option.

Notice that at no point am I saying to stop feeling whatever it is you are feeling. Your emotions are tools. They tell you important things. They are valid except when they are not because something is physically wrong. But even then, it is telling you something.

Once you become consciously aware of your emotions, you can choose not to act on them. You do not have to always act on them. You actually have a choice on how to respond. But you can only get to that point by becoming aware of your emotions, labeling them, and intellectually distancing yourself a bit so that you feel the feelings but have space to decide what to do about it. When you get to this point after a few months of practice, you will realize that you have a super power. You will no longer be on emotional response autopilot. You will now be free to choose your response instead of just responding. This will allow you to choose to respond strategically.

Please note that everyone is different. Some people can do this easily and some cannot. We all come to this with different problems. Some of us have emotional trauma in our background. I, for instance, have PTSD that I have had to (with the help of a professional) train my brain how to cope with so it no longer controls me. That was NOT easy to do but it was doable and I did it. Other people have crippling anxiety and may need medication to cope and that is ok too. The brain is not some magic thing. Consciousness is not magic. It is a physical thing and just like any other part of your physical body, it can malfunction.

Becoming aware of your emotions and brain functions will help you get to a point that you can decide how best to cope in a way that is more beneficial than just being on autopilot and hoping for the best. When your emotions stop controlling you, and you gain the ability to choose your response, you will be free and that is like having a superpower.

Leadership Styles and Impact On Team Dynamics

At this point it should be clear that you cannot really choose a leadership style unless you can choose your responses to the conditions you find yourself in. But it is important to discuss leadership styles because some leadership styles are toxic to your team and some are more empowering. This is a philosophic discussion that is only really possible if you have the ability to choose your response.

CONTROL ISSUES

Some managers want to be the boss. They have a need to be in control. The reality of this style of management is it happens when the manager in question is not in control of themselves. They are on autopilot. They probably have some sort of trauma from a time they were not in control of what was happening to them and they respond by trying to control others. This is why some managers time employee's bathroom breaks.

No one likes working for managers like this. It is toxic. The impact on the team is lost productivity. The team spends so much time managing the boss's insecurities that they do not have the time to get their work done. They really cannot do both. If you have this problem – get help. You will not be able to fix it until you address your emotional insecurities about being in control.

EFFECTIVE MANAGEMENT IS SUPPORTIVE MANAGEMENT

Management is a support function. Managers do not do the work, they support the employees who are doing the work. Their orientation should be helping the team, not using the team to stroke their ego. When employees feel supported, they can get their work done. They feel ok asking for help when they have a problem and productivity rises.

To be this sort of manager, you need to be aware enough to not act out on your insecurities and instead focus on what the individual employees need to do a better job. You need to be able to choose to act in a way that assists your employee. This does not mean you let them walk all over you. It means that you are choosing your response to be strategic about helping and not hurting your employee. I am going to discuss how to use this superpower to protect yourself and your employees from abusive individuals in another chapter. For now, just understand that self awareness is the foundational superpower that allows you to be a good manager instead of a toxic manager on autopilot.

CHAPTER 3: MANAGING CHANGE AND TRANSITIONS

The second superpower is the ability to manage change in yourself and others.

No one likes change. The people who succeed are the ones who are able to control their response to change so they can adapt more readily. The key to being able to do this is to understand why we all resist change and the behavioral science behind how change happens. This knowledge is going to help you manage change in yourself and others more effectively. Knowing this science, how change occurs and how to manage it, is like having a superpower.

Managing Personal Reactions to Change

To recognize and manage your personal reactions to change, it helps to be self aware. Once you can recognize and manage your own personal reactions, you can choose your response more effectively and strategically.

Fortunately, we have science to help us with this. Behavioral modification or change is well studied. We have almost 80 years of research into this topic and the research is very consistent. This means the process by which learning (change) occurs in the brain, and how behaviors are modified is well known and fortunately, it is easy to understand. There is very little deviation in outcomes based on this knowledge.

Remember what I told you about how the brain learns to do new things? You need to repeat the pattern for the brain to learn the pattern. This process takes a little over a month of steady, regular daily practice. The first lesson is that change – even wanted change – is something that is going to take some time to accomplish. It is not going to be easy because our brains resist learning.

Anticipating Resistance to Change

The second thing we know about change processes is that everyone and every animal resists learning whatever it is. It does not matter what it is.

Our brains REALLY like their established patterns and when it is introduced to a new pattern, it does not like it right away. What is happening is that the brain wants the new pattern to fit into the old pattern and when it does not, then the brain may throw a fit. Your brain might decide to be angry, frustrated, mad, sad. It might tell you that you are an idiot when you definitely are not.

Think of your brain as if it is a toddler. Like a toddler that has learned to put a round peg in a round hole, when you give the toddler a square peg, it will probably try to fit the new square peg into the old round hole and get frustrated when it does not fit. Your brain does this, too. Your brain is going to want to go back to its old ways of doing things. You can anticipate this resistance to change and address it by being aware of it. It is not failure – it is a normal part of the learning process.

When it happens in yourself you do not have to beat yourself up for not doing the new thing. You can just say to yourself that the difficulty your brain is having is normal resistance to change. Then just gently nudge the brain to do what you want it to do anyway. Just like it is not helpful to yell at a toddler learning shapes, it is not helpful to yell at your brain or yourself either. Change is hard for everyone. Some people have a harder time than others, but just like practicing becoming self aware will help you become self aware, practicing change will help you change easier, too.

If you are a manager rolling out a new process, anticipate that your staff is going to have difficulties adapting to the change. Plan for it to take some time. Do not get mad that your staff are not robots you can reprogram. Accept that they are humans and have human brains that will resist change just because that is what ALL brains do – they resist change. Give your staff time. Help them practice. Encourage them to practice. Build in micro lessons if you can. Keep the change and the encouragement in front of them for WELL over a month – give them two months ideally. Heck, give yourself two months. It really does take time and practice. It does not require anger to create the change. Just repetition and time. Stick with it.

A Tip for Effective Change Management:

If you can make the old way of doing things not work at all anymore, it will speed up the process. But I do not necessarily recommend doing this because if you eliminate an old way that works and replace it with a new way that does not work at all, you will have bigger problems than just resistance to change.

Sometimes and oftentimes people in workplaces resist change because they have learned that the proposed changes actually do sometimes make things worse.

Rules for Communicating Effectively With Your Team About Change

Rule #1. Do not treat your team like they are idiots or that they are out to make you fail. It is entirely possible they are but if your team hates you that much then there is probably a good reason for that. And that reason would be YOU!

Rule #2. Be sympathetic. Even if you are pretty sure the change will be net good if successful, it is still going to be difficult for your team because you are essentially asking them to rewire their brains. So give them time and space and be sympathetic. Communicate that with them. You understand why they are nervous and may not feel good or that they do not want to change how they do things, and that is ok. The organization needs this anyway so please keep trying.

Rule #3 is the most important rule. Listen to your employees. No one knows what they do not know. You do not know what you do not know. We all have expertise and blind spots. This is especially true of managers who are not doing the actual work but are supporting those who do. Before you even think about creating changes, find out from your team what is working and what is not working before you suggest any changes to anything!

Don't. Change. The. Things. That. Work!!!! Change the things that don't work. Start there. Once you have success on those – THEN – you can start tackling bigger things. Seriously, change the little things first. Acclimating your team to better adapt to change is something they can practice and will benefit from practicing. It is like any other skill. Start small then build on the success. Your brain and their brains will appreciate it. If, as the change process is underway, your staff surfaces a problem then listen to it. Do not assume it is regular resistance until you have listened to the complaint and researched it to ensure YOU are not making a mistake.

Mostly, just be compassionate and patient with yourself and others as they learn new ways of doing and being. Once you can do this and understand it and manage it effectively in yourself, then you can help others with the process. And this will seem like a superpower to those who struggle. But really, it is just science.

CHAPTER 4: TAKING OWNERSHIP

The third superpower is ownership and taking responsibility. Responsibility is the ability to choose your response. This is why self awareness was the first topic and mastering change was the second. Being able to choose your response is a type of change that will take time to learn. But it is essential to becoming an excellent leader.

Ownership in a Humanistic Framework is Service Oriented

Leaders are the people who take responsibility to support others. Even if you are not a manager, if you do this you will be treated as a leader as others look to you and come to you for help. A leader is someone who has chosen to take responsibility to help their teams achieve more. This is how we make sure the work gets done. It is not about doing it yourself. It is about taking ownership of your own choices and decisions and then doing the work needed to effectively support yourself AND others.

Embracing Leadership

A leader is not a boss. A leader is a leader because people WANT to follow them. You cannot just declare yourself a leader. You are chosen by others to lead them. There are a variety of reasons why people choose to follow certain people. Maybe they have better ideas? Maybe they offer the individual a sense of protection? If you want to be a managerial superpower, you need to commit to using your superpowers for good and to help others.

The problem is that the people who are service oriented rarely want to be leaders. It is not like they wake up and think – I should lead people today. Instead, it is other people asking them to lead that makes them a leader. I often joke that I fell into what I do backwards screaming – NOOOOOO! At some point I had to just embrace it. I was being selfish to not help people because that is what was happening. People asking me to lead were asking me to help them. If this happens to you then embrace it. Be helpful. Understand that if people are tapping you to be in a leadership position it is because they see the necessary superpower of a leader in you which is compassion.

Compassion is a Superpower!

Compassion is surprisingly rare and difficult to act on in daily life. It is not that people do not want compassion. People are HUNGRY for it. It is that most people do not have enough control over their responses to their emotions and so they are not able to choose to be compassionate in difficult situations. Those that can choose to be compassionate in difficult situations seem like superheroes to everyone else.

To recap what we've learned so far: practicing self awareness allows you to practice changing your responses to your emotions, which allows you to choose your response. So choose your response wisely and strategically and choose to be compassionate. The people who others want to follow are the ones who choose to respond with compassion. Yes, this takes A LOT of practice. So much practice. It is insanely difficult to respond to difficult and scary situations with compassion. It absolutely requires practice.

When I start teaching compassion as a superpower, people reject the idea. Lots of people see being compassionate as weak. In reality, choosing your response is NOT weak – it is powerful. Not everyone can do this. When you choose compassion, you choose responses that benefit yourself and others.

What I think is really happening when people resist compassion is that people want to feel their emotions. They want to justify their lashing out because they feel horrible. I get it. But a good manager does not lash out – they fix problems! They do not make things worse. They FIX PROBLEMS – including their own. They do not let people walk all over them. Instead, they use compassion to de-escalate situations and reframe situations so that good comes out of what might truly be a horrible situation. In other words, they stay calm under pressure and act strategically and compassionately to ensure good outcomes for everyone including themselves. It is a superpower to be able to do this. Seriously, it is.

People who can wield compassion rise to whatever challenges they face with grace and dignity. It is really that powerful. People who can do this have LEARNED to do this by practicing it. No one is born knowing how to do this. The people who can choose to respond with compassion are sought out as leaders.

Setting Performance Standards and Fostering Team Development

How does learning to respond to difficult situations with compassion help you set performance standards and foster team development?

It helps because instead of dictating arbitrary standards, you are listening to what the real problems are and figuring out solutions that help everyone. Performance standards are the solutions to help make sure the work is done and it is done well.

I am going to let you in on a little secret. All work is collaborative. All of it. In order for work to get done on a team, they have to collaborate. The better they collaborate, the more effective the team is.

Fostering compassion for everyone on the team will help them collaborate better. Having compassion for people who are resisting or having trouble with colleagues will help them get through whatever it is, with grace and dignity. You cannot help your team if you are not compassionate with the individuals ON your team. The more you do this then the more it becomes the social norm and the more it fosters team cohesion and development.

Again, I am totally aware that there are sometimes individuals who are bullies in our workspaces. I have made a career out of teaching people the science of how to make them stop. But most people are not bullies and even if they are, approaching everyone with compassion is going to help you solve that. Again, I will go into more on how to do this in the next chapter which is about handling conflict.

Balancing Organizational Goals With Individual Needs

A compassionate approach to everyone does require you to balance organizational goals with individual needs. To have an effective team focused on organizational goals, you need to treat the individual with dignity and worth.

The ONLY way to find balance between the needs of the organization and the needs of the individuals on your team is to have compassion for the members of your team. They are not robots. They are full fledged humans with a host of human problems.

It is the job of the leader to balance the needs of the whole against the needs of the individuals. That is part of the manager's job. It is probably the most difficult part of the job. Usually because there are no ideal solutions where everyone wins. Compassion for the whole and compassion for the individual will help you make those difficult decisions in the best way you can. It will help you communicate the needs of the whole to any individual who just is not working out. Often those conversations end up in amicable separation.

Compassion is a superpower. You get there by practicing self awareness and then practicing choosing compassion even, and especially, when it is hard. Embracing compassion will cause you to end up in leadership roles and you need to be prepared for that.

~~~~~

CHAPTER 5: CONFLICT MANAGEMENT

The fourth superpower is conflict management. This is the chapter where I promised I would talk about dealing with difficult people or bullies.

Managing people is difficult. Mostly because we humans are not robots and we rarely agree. Understanding how to manage conflict and turn conflict into collaboration is a key skill. It is at the heart of humanistic management. Your self awareness, the science of change, and you taking responsibility for your side of the interaction, is going to help you learn how to deal with conflicts with dignity and grace. Behavioral science is going to help you learn how to do this well. Once you know this, it is like having a superpower. This knowledge will change everything about how you approach people, disagreements, and deal with conflict among your team.

Recognizing Personal Conflict Management Tendencies

Managing conflict well starts with managing your own response to conflict. We are humans. Disagreements can trigger lots of things in lots of people and you are not immune from this.

Some people have trauma from their childhood. Some are anxiety prone. Our brains often treat conflict as a life or death situation which hinders our ability to respond sanely to a situation in which we are not actually in danger of getting eaten. To start this, I want you to spend some time thinking about how you personally respond to conflict. What are the patterns you fall into? Check in with yourself. If you can recognize patterns, that is great, it means you are on your way to changing those patterns using the science we talked about earlier regarding how to change how you respond to things.

It is ok if you do not respond well to certain situations. We all have days when we feel better and days when we do not. If you have something traumatic going on in other parts of your life, like a family member is sick or died recently, you cannot be expected to respond ideally to the things around you. What I want you to try to do is to become aware of your responses and when you become aware then try to choose a different response. Ideally, one based in compassion for yourself and for the person you think you are in conflict with.

Sometimes that has to be done after the fact. I do this after the fact all the time. When my anxiety gets the best of me, I am not at my best because I am not totally in control of how I am responding. Afterwards, when I am calmer and recognize that I fell into a pattern that was not ideal, I will attempt to invoke compassion and decide on the best way to fix the problem. Then, I go back to the individual I was not behaving my best with and apologize. I tell them that I was not in a good place and that my response was not about them. It was about me and I would like to work with them to resolve whatever it is and solve the problem. Usually, this is met with appreciation and thanks. Most people understand. They are human too and they might not have been at their best either. When this happens to me, I ask for a reset.

Once you get good at this or better than you were, then you can start helping your team with this. You model the humility of not being perfect and encourage others to do the same. Encourage everyone to give people grace to be flawed. Mostly, it is about the desire to fix the problem and treat people with compassion and dignity. This is hard and it requires us to reset when we fail.

Using Behavioral Science to De-escalate Conflicts

There is a difference between disagreements and conflicts. Some people treat disagreement as a conflict and if you do this, then stop. Work on becoming aware and de-escalate yourself!

A disagreement is when there is a problem to solve and we do not agree on the best way to solve it. The solution to a disagreement is to collaborate and learn from one another and work on a joint solution that takes into account the best ideas from everyone. A disagreement is rational and can be discussed rationally.

A conflict is not rational. A conflict is a disagreement that becomes protracted to the point of inaction. The disagreement stops being a disagreement – ie: something rational we can talk about and work out - and starts becoming something more personal. It is something that you want to win instead of resolve.

In a workplace, having employees who do not want to resolve disagreements is counterproductive to getting things done. Conflicts can happen between people, between groups, and within groups. They are productivity killers. Your job as a manager is to de-escalate conflicts so that the disagreements can be resolved and work can resume. Yes, this is part of any manager's job. If you fail to do this then you fail as a manager.

Learn how to de-escalate yourself first. Then you can apply these skills and teach and coach your team to do the same. Most people are capable of doing this and want to have better relationships and be in less conflict. Most people want to learn this!

There are, however, people who thrive on conflict or who see everything as a battle to be won. If people fail to de-escalate their conflicts, you may need to let them go. But do not make any assumptions about who is doing what and who is responsible for what. Your first approach should be to encourage and teach collaboration as a way to deal with disagreements and to de-escalate conflicts into problems that can be collaboratively solved. The science is the same as the science of change. It just takes repetition of the new social norms for them to be established. People will resist. They may be personally invested in the conflict and see it as a moral battle to be won.

What you need to do as a manager is to not accept bad behavior. Conflicts are not really a problem unless they result in inappropriate behavior. People in conflict will justify their conflict and their lack of desire to work with others.

Bullying and harassment really do occur in workplaces and the people engaging in this behavior rationalize why they do it. So your approach needs to do 2 things at once:

- Encourage collaboration and de-escalation
- Make it so someone who is engaging in bullying/harassment or passive aggressively withholding resources cannot do that anymore

You need to do both at once.

A third note. Victims of bullying are often made out to be the problem by the bully. So do not assume you know who the problem is. Just note that there is a problem to be solved and it is your job as a manager to help solve it. You will not know who is telling the truth or if both are telling the truth until you learn more.

Radical Transparency

Here is the process that works for me and that is based in this science: radical transparency. This is a term I learned from Harit Nagpal, the CEO of Tata

Play. He has his teams engage in radical transparency whenever there is a conflict so that they can de-escalate the conflict and collaborate to get the work done. I have used this technique my entire working life to de-escalate conflicts, establish good working relationships, and to get rid of bullies, which is icing on the cake.

Transparency requires compassion and rational thought to do, which is how you de-escalate conflicts and turn them into collaborations. It also makes it so anyone bullying or being passive aggressive cannot hide because everything is transparent. I do this not to out bullies. I do not assume anyone is a bully until they prove to me that they are. Instead, I view this as something professionals do. If there is a misunderstanding, let's clear it up so we can get moving again.

Basically, I document everything. Every conversation. If I have a verbal conversation with someone I am having trouble dealing with, I follow up with an email to confirm my understanding of what we just discussed. Who is doing what, what the timelines are, everything. I CC my manager so they are in the loop. I assume maybe the problem was my understanding of what they said and I am working to fix my end of the problem. My goal is to reset the relationship so that we can both get our work done. I assume that they are well meaning. Most of the time they are. I can count the number of people who respond badly to this on one hand and it is not even a full hand. Only three people over the course of my working life did not respond well to this. Usually what happens is the person I was having a problem with and I become allies going forward as trust is built through transparency.

Again, this is about me choosing to de-escalate myself so that I do not turn a disagreement into a conflict. If I find myself thinking of other people as enemies to be vanquished, I need to de-escalate! When I de-escalate myself, I can professionally respond with compassion for myself and others to figure out if there is a disagreement or a miscommunication and if there is, I solve it so that I can work collaboratively with my colleagues. Most of the time this is welcomed, as the other person was struggling with the interaction, too. I take ownership of my part to fix it because that is what professionals do. My mother always said that it takes two people to fight and she is right. When I stop fighting, the conflict almost always goes away.

Dealing with Bullying and Harassment

There is an exception to my mother's rule. It takes two people to fight, except when one of them is abusive. Let's talk about how this process works for people who are not acting in good faith.

It turns out that the process of radical transparency outs them. For people who are well intentioned, radical transparency grounded in compassion aids and encourages collaboration. People who are not well intentioned or who bully and harass others, will not respond well to radical transparency at all. That is on them. You cannot force someone who is not capable of working well with others to work well with others. It does not matter why they are behaving the way they are. It is not your job as a manager to diagnose anyone else's mental life.

All you can do is encourage people, with compassion, to collaborate and be transparent about the work requests and where things stand and what problems come up and what agreements are reached about the work. If someone refuses to collaborate and refuses to treat their colleagues with dignity and professionalism, it will become obvious. As your collaborative culture is being adopted, it will become clear who is a good fit for the team and who is not. It will also be clear if someone is being abusive – that they are being abusive. What I tell my team is to CC me on all communications if there is a problem happening in the communication. If someone is rude or denigrates a colleague, I do not tolerate that. We have a discussion and if they keep doing it then I let them go.

If they are unable to meet their deadlines or provide needed resources to other members of the team then I discuss this with them. Are they having trouble getting the resources? What do we need to do to fix the workflow? Are they waiting on someone else to get their work done? I do not assume they are a problem – I work collaboratively and openly with them to solve the problem they are experiencing. I support them because bullies often sabotage the work of their victims and I do not know who is the victim and who is the bully or whether they are just having difficulties communicating. That is why I treat everyone with compassion.

What I do not do is tolerate name calling or gossip or any rationalization for work not getting done that is conflict and not factual or rational.

If there is an interpersonal conflict or someone behaving badly, let your staff know that you expect them to be professional and that they should work through their disagreements with dignity and compassion. If there is a problem with someone behaving badly, you will handle it. In the meantime, you need them to be radically transparent about the work and they need to treat everyone, including the person they have a problem with, with dignity and as a respected colleague.

If it turns out someone on your team really is a bully then they will not be able to behave professionally nor will they be able to treat their colleagues with dignity. Do not assume you know who is a problem before you start this. I get called into companies to help with this and it is not unusual for the person I am told is the problem to actually be a victim of bullying by someone else who is sabotaging them.

What I want you to understand is that a conflict just tells you that there is a problem that needs to be solved. Treat everyone with dignity and compassion and request they do the same. Demand they do the same. Ask for transparency in all interactions and documentation and what is really happening will become clear.

Do not go into this with any assumptions and do not believe the bad-mouthing people in conflict do when they are in conflict. Just shut disparaging comments down and let them know that it is not acceptable or professional to talk about their colleagues that way and that you expect them to behave professionally and with dignity even if the other person does not. Keep reinforcing that as part of a change process and eventually this will resolve itself and any problem people will become clear and you can eliminate them.

Developing Effective Conflict Resolution Skills

It starts with you. Learn to de-escalate yourself first. Treat every member of your team with dignity and compassion.

Make dignity and professionalism the core expectation for interpersonal interactions and reinforce this frequently. Be sure to model this behavior for your team. If you do not do this then neither will they. When there is a problem, encourage collaboration and transparency so that the problem can be solved. Encourage team members to de-escalate and collaborate instead. Keep an eye out for people who are not treating their colleagues with dignity and coach them to help them improve.

When a problem does arise, ask for radical transparency and professionalism and that you expect every member of the team to be treated with dignity. If someone is abusive to their colleagues and refuses to collaborate, have a conversation about whether they should continue or not with your organization. Basically, treat every conflict as an opportunity for collaboration. Treat everyone with dignity and compassion, especially those who are under stress and not behaving optimally.

If you do this, you will effectively resolve most conflicts and de-escalate them. The bonus is that this approach is going to help you deal more effectively with difficult personalities who often just need to be treated with dignity. And if it turns out someone is a bully or actively harassing or sabotaging their colleagues - you will learn that too. As you practice this, you will understand why it is a superpower.

CHAPTER 6: MANAGING PEOPLE

Finally, the fifth superpower is the ability to manage people and personalities. The previous superpowers were all leading up to this skill.

Humanistic management is about managing real live humans. It is no easy task. To manage people, you need to be self aware, you need to be able to choose your response, and adapt to change effectively and strategically. You need to take ownership of your actions and choose your actions wisely. You need to know how to manage conflict in a compassionate and scientific way so that your choices work.

All of that is going to help you manage people and whatever personalities you have to deal with – with grace and dignity. You will not just be flopping around hoping for the best and failing. You will be a master of people management. This is where everything you have learned so far comes together and gets applied to your role as a manager. It all starts with being able to manage yourself. If you are not in control of your behavior choices then difficult people can manipulate you which is not good.

Choosing to act with dignity and compassion is going to help you be the respected professional you want to be. You act with dignity when you treat other people with dignity. I find it is easiest to do that when I actively choose to feel compassion for difficult people. Often, the only thing that difficult people really need to de-escalate themselves is to be treated with dignity and compassion. This really is a super power.

When I do classes and I do a unit on compassion, the next week people come in and tell me that it changed everything. They were skeptical but it changed everything. And it does. First, it changes how you respond. This in turn changes how people respond to you. It does not fix everything, but it fixes an enormous amount. For the situations it does not fix, it helps you not be bothered by them as much.

I want you to envision a dignified person dealing with a difficult person. Are they angry? Mad? Calm? Serene? They are calm and serene, right? Now I want you to think about past interactions you have had with people you felt were wonderful and dignified. Did they demean you? Dehumanize you? Or did they make you feel seen and did they treat you with dignity? You know the answer is that they treated you kindly and with dignity. Practice this. It really will change how you respond to everything and help you make choices that will benefit yourself and others.

When it comes to dealing with difficult people and even bullies, treating them with dignity will both disarm them and make it clear to everyone witnessing the interaction where the problem really lies. How does it disarm them? A calm reaction is NOT what a bully wants. Someone insulting you wants you to react. By not reacting, you eliminate their reward. The other thing this does is it helps bystanders understand that what is happening is not a conflict, it is a one sided harassment. You cannot convince people that someone else is behaving badly by behaving badly yourself. You can only do that by remaining calm while the other person behaves badly.

Imagine a scenario where you see two people on the street. In one scenario, they are yelling at each other. In the other, only one person is yelling and the other is standing there not saying anything. When you see two people yelling, you assume both are a problem. When you see only one person yelling, you think something is wrong with the out-of-control yeller and you feel sympathy for their target. Remaining calm makes it so that other people do not assume you are part of the problem. They can clearly see the other person is not in control of their behavior.

When you deal with difficult people, do not make any assumptions about why they are behaving that way. You do not know what is going on. Just treat them with dignity, work on resolving whatever the problem is, and move on.

An Example

Let me give you an example. I was at a car rental place and the guy in front of me was yelling at the clerk. The clerk was processing his rental. The man was upset that his car was in the shop and he needed a rental at all. This was not the clerk's fault. He could not help the guy solve his car repair problem. All he could do is help this guy rent a car. He did not try to get the guy to stop yelling. He simply, quietly and professionally, got the paperwork together so this angry man could rent a car. It was a masterful example of how to do it right. He did not engage. He did not fight back. He just solved the problem professionally and treated the man who was yelling at him with dignity and compassion. When I got up to him I complimented him. He told me that this guy was clearly just having a bad day and all he could do was help him.

This is what dignity and compassion looks like in action in a workplace. You are not responsible for the choices others make. You are responsible for how you choose to respond. And when you choose to respond with dignity and compassion, you are responding in a professional manner. This approach is going to help you build strong relationships with team members and it will encourage strong relationships among team members. After all, who do you want to work with? Someone who is angry all the time or someone who treats you with dignity and compassion? Be the manager you want.

To help your team, you need to encourage and help them practice these skills. All new skills take time to learn and practice and that requires time and patience. Give your staff the time and support they need to improve in these areas so they can be super managers too and learn to manage themselves as well. Mostly, be supportive. Help your team learn what they need to not only do their job well, but to help them grow in their careers. Root for them to succeed. Help them succeed and help them become the best versions of themselves so they can.

CHAPTER 7: LEADING BY EXAMPLE

The key to learning these 5 superpowers is practice. You have to practice them to learn them.

You teach them to your team, not by bringing them the latest leadership coaching fad, but by actually practicing these skills yourself in front of them. Nothing impacts your team more than you responding to difficult situations and difficult people with professionalism rooted in compassion and watching you treat people with dignity. It really is that powerful.

If you are not there yet then start practicing this. As you improve, your relationships will improve, and your staff will take notice and start imitating you. We humans learn most by imitation. Do not underestimate the power of your example. As you improve, and only once you improve, can you start coaching members of the team on how to create a positive inclusive team culture. The only way to have a positive inclusive team culture is for everyone to treat everyone else with dignity. Compassion helps us forgive the occasional transgression and prevents it from escalating into conflict. Caring for one another is what makes a team culture positive. It is foundational to everything else, especially inclusion. Collaboration requires inclusion of everyone. Anyone being excluded is being prevented from collaborating and working.

It also means that anyone engaging in exclusion by gossiping, bullying, harassment, or passive-aggressive withholding, is actively sabotaging your attempts to create a positive inclusive team culture. So deal with any problem that arises by asking for transparency and remind everyone of your expectation that they treat their colleagues with dignity and compassion. Anyone who does not treat colleagues with dignity needs to be talked to and coached, and if that fails, a separation or firing may be required.

Mostly, I want to emphasize that this is about practicing self care for yourself. Compassion for others is self care for yourself. It will help you not respond to negativity that comes your way. Because instead of being upset, you are going to respond by wondering what is going on that this person in this workplace is not behaving professionally. Something is wrong and they need help. That response is very, very, very self protective. Once you practice it then you will see why. I understand it is counterintuitive, but there is a reason every major religion and philosopher throughout history has taught compassion. It is a superpower.

Finally, if you are not a perfect manager – that is ok. No one is. All we can ever do at any time is our best. To do and be better requires practice. Be compassionate with yourself, understand you are a work in progress, keep practicing, and eventually you will become the self-aware professional whose first response to any difficulty is to respond with dignity and compassion. Most of the time anyway.

Top

CHAPTER 8: PRACTICAL APPLICATION AND IMPLEMENTATION

None of this is easy. In order to learn these skills you need to apply them. And as I said at the beginning, this takes practice.

To develop an action plan to apply these concepts to your workplace, start with a single concept and practice it until it becomes second nature. Do not demand people start doing this and get upset when they do not. Work on it yourself first. If you think you are reasonably self aware then start working on ownership and conflict or start working on reminding yourself to respond with dignity and compassion. As you learn these, the next skill will become easier.

You can encourage your staff to check in with their own emotions and help them choose a response that will be beneficial to them, to their colleagues, and to the company. This is all about practice. No one is perfect at this – not even people who have been practicing these skills for a long time. Just encourage practice on compassion, collaboration, and dignity. After a period of adjustment, things will get easier and better.

To integrate these managerial superpowers into your daily management practices, again, it is about practice. Choose one to work on at a time, integrate fully, and then add another. This is what science says works to create lasting change in yourself and others. If you check in with yourself regularly, you can evaluate how you are doing and how you might adjust your strategies. Maybe plan one day a week where you give yourself a ½ hour to assess yourself against your current learning objectives for these various skills. Remember, it is ok to not be good at these things. It is about practice not perfection. Some of these skills yield immediate results like practicing compassion with difficult people and difficult situations. Others take more time to see results.

As you become aware of how you are responding, give yourself compassion for the difficult emotions you are experiencing and then choose to extend your compassion to the other person or persons. Then see what happens. People report to me that this has an immediate effect. But they still have to practice it regularly and remind themselves regularly to choose compassion to make this a habit – something they can do almost automatically. Until you practice it regularly, for a month or two, it will not become a habit. So practice. A word of caution, though. What you practice becomes a habit. So make sure that the things you practice are positive and not negative, otherwise you will end up with bad habits.

~~~~

CHAPTER 9: CONCLUSION AND KEY TAKEAWAYS

To conclude, no one wants to work for a bad manager. Bad managers negatively impact productivity. If you are going to be a manager of people, learn how to do it well. That means you need to learn how to deal with various people while meeting them where they are, including people who are difficult. To do that, you need to know how to manage and de-escalate conflict and turn it into collaborations. You need to know how to shut down abusive individuals so that they do not harm you or your team and you need to learn how to do that with dignity, compassion, and professionalism.

To do that, you need to take ownership of yourself and your responses so that you can choose your responses so you respond optimally instead of in a knee-jerk fashion. You need to understand how to train yourself to change so that you can master change in yourself and others so that you can choose your responses. This requires you to be self aware enough to recognize how you are responding so that you can make different choices.

Reflect on your own personal leadership strengths and weaknesses, and practice becoming aware of your responses so that you can choose different responses. Then, practice it so that you can grow into the leader you want to be.

Further Opportunities

I realize I went through a lot of these topics superficially – giving you the high level takeaways for each topic. The reality is, to learn the science of change management is its own 1-hour course.

I have multiple courses on various aspects of dealing with conflicts and bullying and harassment situations using science and dignity. I have programs that go into depth on the philosophy of humanistic leadership and management. If you want deeper dives and more information, check out my other course and book options, which I have listed in the next chapter.

But the most important thing you can do is to decide you want to improve and then practice,

practice, practice. Good luck. The more you practice self awareness, the more you will be able to interrupt your old habits and replace them with better, more effective ones.

~~~~~

CHAPTER 10: ABOUT THE AUTHOR

Jennifer Hancock is the author of several best-selling and award-winning books and is the founder of *Humanist Learning Systems*. Not only was she raised as a Humanist, she is considered one of the top speakers and writers in the world of Humanism today. Her professional background is varied including leadership positions in both the for-profit and non-profit sectors.

She teaches Humanism – a combination of Love, Rationality, Science, and Responsibility. Her courses will give you hope. It will help you simplify your life by reducing the complexity of the problems you face, which will in turn help you reduce your anxiety. Finally, because this is all science based, it will work.

What makes her unique is that she teaches humanistic approaches grounded in dignity and compassion, coupled with science-based behavioral modification techniques to create positive workplace cultures that eliminate unwanted behaviors like bullying, harassment, and discrimination, while positively reinforcing the behaviors you do want.

Ms. Hancock has a BA in Liberal Studies from the University of Hawaii at Manoa (1990). Her field of study combined cognitive linguistics, anthropology, and psychology. While in college, she apprenticed as a dolphin trainer for a dolphin language/cognition laboratory which is where she learned the behavioral science and behavior modification techniques she now teaches.

Ms. Hancock has worked in executive leadership roles her entire career (since graduating college in 1990). She has literally never not worked in leadership/management. In the course of her career, she has provided training to companies all over the world for both executive leadership as well as staff. She started training and coaching staff in her first job out of college as the director of volunteer services for the Los Angeles SPCA, and has provided training, support, and mentoring programs at every job she's held since, including her stint as the manager of acquisition group information for a 1/2 billion dollar company.

She has over 30 years of experience working in executive leadership and in providing leadership and management training to others. If you let her, she can teach you how to be a more authentic and effective leader who is both powerfully ethical and armed with the technical skills required to master whatever challenges you face with grace and dignity.

Check out her courses and books below to see how she can help you.

More Learning from Jennifer Hancock

OTHER BOOKS BY JENNIFER HANCOCK

- Applied Humanism: How to Create More Ethical and Effective Businesses
- Humanistic Conflict Management
- The Humanist Approach to Happiness

- Jen Hancock's Handy Humanism Handbook
- The Bully Vaccine
- The Humanist Approach to Grief and Grieving
- How to Win Arguments Without Arguing
- Ending Harassment & Retaliation in the Workplace
- Why Bullies Bully & How to Stop Them Using Science
- Reality-Based Decision Making for Effective Strategy Development
- How to De-escalate Conflicts Using Behavioral Science
- Why Conflict Management Doesn't Work
- How to Prevent Passive Aggressive People from Wreaking Havoc in the Workplace
- How to Handle Cranky Customers
- How to Humanistically Handle Bad Bullying Bosses

- Why is Change so Hard?
- Planning for Personal Success

Courses Taught by Jennifer Hancock

- Workplace Bullying for HR professionals
- Living Made Simpler
- An Introduction to Humanism
- Socratic Jujitsu: How to Win Arguments Without Argument
- Why Conflict Resolution Doesn't Work When the Problem is Bullying
- Bridging the Generational Divide: Millennials vs. Boomers
- Ending Harassment and Retaliation in the Workplace
- Reality-Based Decision Making for Effective Strategy Development
- How to De-escalate Conflicts Using Behavioral Science
- Why is Change so Hard?

- Principles of Humanistic Management
- 7 Sins of Staff Management
- How to Handle Cranky Customer Problems
- New Manager Orientation
- Humanist Group Leadership Lessons
- Sexual Harassment Training That Works – General
- Sexual Harassment Training That Works – AB 1825
- Stop Bullying in our Workplace – Staff Training
- Sexual Harassment Compliance Training
- No Fear Act Training
- Planning for Personal Success!
- Talking to Your Child About Death
- The Bully Vaccine Toolkit
- How to Talk to Your Child's School About Bullying

- Why Bullies Bully & How to Stop Them
- Humanistic Conflict Management
- Applied Humanistic Leadership

~~~~~

The End

#####

www.ingramcontent.com/pod-product-compliance
Lightning Source LLC
Chambersburg PA
CBHW070358230526
45471CB00006B/2619